Boiling
Point

Boiling Point

Priscilla Hadley

Boiling Point

First Edition, 2025

ISBN: 979-8-9994058-0-7

Library of Congress Control Number: 2025942329

Printed in the United States of America

To those whom I love.

Contents

"En art comme en amour, l'instinct suffit."

"In art as in love, the instinct suffices."

— Anatole France

✧ A NOTE TO THE READER ✧

These words were stitched in order—
one breath leading to the next.

Allow it to unravel the way
grief does—
the way memory does—
not in fragments,
but in flow.

You are not just reading poems,
you are walking a shoreline,
one misstep, and you may miss
the footprints.

—Priscilla

Prologue

It is by no means an irrational fancy that, in a future existence,

we shall look upon what we think our present existence,

as a dream.

—Edgar Allen Poe

———————

What were you dreaming about?

I'd like to take your breath away,
but that power is beyond me.
It lingers on the edge of sleep—
where dreams brush against reality,
where breath is stolen, and time
dissolves.

Words spill from lips,
ink bleeds through thought,
but every word is a lie,
spoken with the certainty of truth.

Why must the line between sleeping and waking
sever me from the life I long to live?

I walk that line,
stumbling over my yearning sea.

Even when someone offers an oar,
I cling to the thought—
my dreams—oh, my dreams—are just before me.

So I wait for night.
I tarry with the moon and her stars,
warring against sleep,
knowing when I wake,
I'll carry the bushel weight of what I left
behind—
in the night, and in the day,
haunted by those
still rolling sand over their souls.

And yet,
sleep is kind to me.
That is why I write—

as the apple scraped of its flesh.
As hope tucked in the pocket of a robe.
—Nevertheless—
I rot. Slowly.

Your dreams, your words—
a death I welcome.

Though my mind whispers soft, cruel doubts,
I cling to dreams still just before me.

I want to fall in love with reality—
but I will never get over my dreams.

Here is my parable.
Here is my summary—

Existing is not for the faint of heart.
Waking up is not for the weak.

And I am losing my balance
between strength
and surrender.

Still

reverie (n.)— a pleasant daydream.

Dum spiro, spero.

While I breathe, I hope.

—Latin Proverb

Fly, fly little birdie,

Rest in your nest with your worm

Taken and torn from its hole in the soil.

While I see you fly fly fly,

I cannot help but think

How beautiful you are to me,

With your brave sunrise hunt.

Whilst in my grave,

I remember, I remember

That little worm was my friend.

Alone in the soil I now lie

With your cry of delight I wonder,

If I should be delighted too?

Though dreams paint the edges of my
days,
I walk the streets where the sun's rays
still burn,
and in the ache of flesh and bone,
I find the truths no dream returns.

I sing in fictional tongue,

yet you understand my every word.

It moves through us,

an ancient dance,

bare feet thudding earth, dust rising.

Indeed, you know the script of my heart,

but you do not act.

You are true.

So my mind will keep

dancing in the flicker of night,

whilst I hum to my firefly

arise, arise

meet me in the light.

Your luminescence flickers,

like golden starlight,

then flicks,

then disappears into the night.

Are you afraid of light?

Oh, lovely,

listen to my song.

Pledge always to stay

if not in the light,

then in the darkness of night,

where we reign.

Like dawn's slow crawl,

love's first breath is warm.

Am-

The Latin root pulled though the soil is brittle,

Am- comes from *Amare*

amare meaning:

To love.

To love, though your roots are malnourished,

To love, even when there is pain.

But love is more than meaning.

It is choosing—

Amare quamquam in tenebris vivis,

To love even though you live in darkness,

Nam cor lucem portat.

For the heart carries the light.

—

In amore sum.

I am in love.

My heart is cracked

just enough,

agape just enough,

for your love

to plant its seed

and bloom throughout my body.

New love,

soft rain on dry earth,

a smile to cracked skin.

The allure of a new season:

First, the healing shower,

a slow, steady bloom,

then the sowing and reaping

to keep the blessing alive.

The sensation of falling out of a plane,

breaking through clouds,

pulling the parachute,

only for it to be tangled and torn—

That is loving you.

Falling with no chance of survival,

but, you still jump.

Loving you doesn't hurt me.

For seven whole minutes

I can fly—

Still

I sip you once and I am drunk.

You are my hangover,

and my cure.

The sound of violins decorates your speech.

Oh, a whole orchestra announces your arrival.

Conducting the passage of time,

going past like light,

and down like fine wine by the fire.

Still

I knew you were different
when my only complaint was my mind
growling for more of you.

You are too fleeting to ignore,

too impressive to enshrine,

Oh, love!

Why are you so cruel?

Honest heaven,

a cool sip from the chalice of longing,

a sigh spilled from the soul.

You must see—

you are what I crave in silence,

and in sleep.

You are all I dream.

You, with the watercolor mind,
water my page with drops of you.

Each spill shifts the hues—
mixing your colors,
melting into mine.

Let me paint what I see.
Let me show how my eyes interpret
your smile.

You are everything I've ever wanted—
and I'll wait,
patiently,
as you prepare your canvas for me.

Add me to your painting,

you,
with your watercolor,
beautiful mind.

Still

Your name tastes like communion,

yet not of grape nor brine—

of copper

and orange.

When the world falls extinct

one thing that will never die is the cry of love.

Still

Words inspire me more than people,
but when people use the right words,
they're unstoppable.

You use your words to caress my soul—
I feel you trace my mind
with nothing but your voice.
The mere thought of you
renders me speechless,

but my eyes follow the curves of your lips,
as honey drips from within you,
filling my ears
while I soak up every drop.

If you're ever lucky
to hear the right words,
it's enough to break your heart—
knowing one day
their words will be forgotten.

But with people like that,

the wind never forgets.

They are carried through the

four corners,

sung by the birds

and lilacs past due.

You are enough to make the world weep.

It longs to hear you speak—

As do I.

I personally always want to overflow your cup.

Never let your glass go dry.

You don't say I love you outright—
you tuck hair behind my ear,
and whisper my name like a prayer.

Still

Freed from the flowers' bend, I plant my feet
And nail them to hold the solid ground.
I walk the final mile of sorrow's heat—
The sun burns through my body, tightly bound.

The roots I tear still cling with desperate will,
Their tendrils twist about my heavy knees.
I cry, yet find the fields are deathly still.
No breeze remains to answer or to tease.

Yet in the ache, I feel the soil sing,
A distant hum that pulls me to the deep.
The petals rot, but still their scents will cling—
Even the dead leave stains where they once ran to weep.

The scent of longing, ever bittersweet.
Lo, I fall bound, yet still bow at your feet.

Boiling Point

If night turned day,

and day turned night,

I wouldn't notice—

not when your laughter is the light,

and your love for me the night.

Hold my hands.

Hold my body.

Hold my heart.

But when you hold my gaze,

I melt—

a puddle of longing at your feet.

You say nothing—

but in the silence,

I hear everything.

The eons will end,

bit by bit I will spread the word that you—

you are the face of romance,

the body of each description of love.

The question is not how many years I'd give.

It's how many years have I lost without feeling my heart

beating?

How many hours of misery have been caused by life

without you?

I follow the seasons.

You are my spring,

my summer,

my autumn,

my winter.

And in you, I smell snow.

I steal flowers

and braid the earth's hair.

In you, I taste life—

dipped in black honey,

seeped in black garlic cloves.

In you, I see light

on cracked glass—

the glass we raised

when I told you I loved you,

the one that shattered today,

filled with fig wine—

if there is such a thing.

I swaddle my love

in a blanket of golden willow.

And I will continue to braid,

and steal,

and taste,

and smell—

until.

Until everything all at once

tilts and spills like

paint, or rum—

and stains the blanket

of golden willow.

If there is such a thing

as golden willow.

Cast silver bullets upon me—

for only then will my love fall.

Not time, nor silence,

can sever what you stirred in me.

I am the Louvre,

you, my Renaissance painting—

inhabiting my whole being,

a work of art, stroked by the hands of God.

I memorize you,

ignoring every other exhibition.

I trace each detail with my eyes,

afraid to blink—

afraid to lose even a second of you.

The sun's love turns your eyes to pools of honey,

spilling warmth across my face when you gaze at me.

I ask our Maker,

which of the angels inspired

Him to make you?

Stained with the juice of the ripest cherries

and the deepest beets,

your lips part, releasing the sweetest sounds,

dripping into me—

and with each word you speak,

the world falls away.

The night sky steals its depth from your hair,

the moon borrows its glow from your smile.

I fall to my knees,

the stars bowing beside me at your feet.

Completely captivated,

I surrender—

my masterpiece,

my muse.

But the museum is closing now.

They dim the lights, whispering to shut the doors.

Tonight, I will find you in my dreams,

where the gallery never closes.

And when morning comes,

I will admire you again—

bathed in the light of a new day.

Still

Terrified,

stupefied,

mortified—

by you

and what you've done to my mind.

But what's even more troubling

is how you took my heart

and engraved your perfect self into it.

A beautiful love.

Stand.

I will speak—

Are you sure it's worth

Your soul?

A story only we can write

or end—

Love, the craving we cradle.

The ache we dress in hope.

May it meet us one day,

I'd like to shake its hand,

to ask why the most beautiful thing

to exist,

is the hardest to find,

and keep.

You are my enemy.

When all I craved was to lie in the field

and breathe my last,

you pulled me to my feet,

and breathed desire into my lungs.

For that I loathe you.

For that alone, I love you.

You are what I crave, as pollen

craves the flower's heart.

To be loved like ferment loves the grapes of the vine is to know fully and wholeheartedly the nature of our existence.

Still

Love is not taken—it's given.

The hand that reaches first,

not to claim but to offer.

Love is no war.

It is the quiet between the earth-shattering

crack,

the life you choose

again and again

to give,

with nothing in return.

When one day,

they place roses on your tomb,

I will run to you in the after.

Walking with you in the next life, too.

Warn me before you tell me you love

me—

so I can take my seat

and nail my feet to the ground.

Lest dead leaves cling again to a dead

tree,

and I fall deeper

and deeper

in admiration of you.

I will decompose in flesh,

but never in love.

Sweeter than strawberry wine.

Let me not regret choosing

desire over sense.

We know what wine does to the spirit

after a season of sorrow.

Still, I wonder

what will become of me,

for you are the richest of wines.

Believe: even in pain,

you live deeper than most.

Believe: even in love,

you ache more than others.

There is nothing to compare love to,

except an endless sky

of falling stars.

A galactic embrace—
running as fast as it can.
Earth opens its arms wide,
welcoming the impact of love.

Fragments collide in small kisses,
knowing they must wait
generations
to meet again.

We call a grand asteroid
a planet destroyer—
and it's true.
There is no love without ruin,
no love to come upon, yet leave
unscathed.

But, still, Earth opens its arms
wide, wide, wide—
and does not move,
not until its final embrace.

I would turn my cheek for you,

bare my soul for you,

give my life to you—

this love I have for you.

You don't even have to say please.

The Garden of Eden is not a place— it is a space between our beings. Cloaked in fruitful labor and light. Let the garden be our greatest delight. We have enough to reap. Our seeds grow, even in the dry seasons of love. And when the sky forgets us, we do not despair—we provoke rain to fall. May it weep for our love, and in doing so, water our vines and our herbs, our sacred ground. If love is a storm, let it take me whole.

Possibly, I will lose you.

Cease to hold your hand,

unable to whisper how much I care.

Beyond all reason,

I love you anyway.

Even when you call me crazy,

for loving you despite.

Even when the world rolls its eyes,

I keep mine on you.

You are not disposable.

You are worth fighting for.

I believe in love.

I believe in us.

Is it the sin in us that limits expression of love?
If for an hour I was without inhibition,
I would spend fifty-nine speaking every untainted
thought limited only by my humanity

—

and one glorious minute kissing you.

Do you desire proof of my intentions?
Truly, I have nothing else to give.

You are the captor of my heart,
the holder of my hands,
the keeper of my peace.

Figuratively,
you hung the stars
for us to sit beneath.
You are what the earth orbits around,
the guard of my house,
delight of my soul.

At any rate,
let this be proof.
Let it be known
by the cherry blossoms
and the world.

Still

Come with me. That's all I ask.

If you walk beside me, I won't care when time ends.

Take my hand over salt fields,

and lavender pasture.

We'll walk along the horizon

until the ocean stops calling our names.

Spin the Heavens with your

insurmountable beauty.

On its axis, the world turns, tangled in

your web

braided and lovely.

Let it be cut—

Lest they mistake you for the

supernatural,

and the angels take you from this earth.

There's a chance.

But baby, please say,

Heaven can wait.

In 409 BC,

a noble runner was sent—

ordered by his empire

to bear the weight of the world,

tasked with the words:

"Victory," I say, "Victory!"

He ran.

The news branded his mind,

burned on his lips,

his body, a vessel of triumph,

feet pounding the earth for 173 miles—

until God Himself declared him to rest,

falling, breathless, to his death.

His last words were delivered:

Victory.

—

I have no news.

I did not conquer the Persians.

I couldn't even conquer my longing.

But I will run to you.

I will run 174 miles to find you,

until my body gives way,

my scored lips declaring

one final decree.

Iris on my grave,

and carved on my plaque:

"Love is my greatest triumph.

Victory, I say—Victory!"

There are essentials.

Bread is one.

But if it were stripped

of its core—ravaged of its meat—

would it still be essential?

You see,

I seek, I ask:

would I wait for rot?

To be scraped of your love for me?

No.

For this is my view

of a life well lived:

Love—

with its flesh

always tender

and fresh.

Truth was there all along—
though she chose to wear
something off, something wrong,
a scarf of white in a sea of red.

You paid no care,
too fixed on the light
with oars hitting the waters bare,
that light,
flitting across the water's hair.

In the end, it is the end.

—

You were my strength
on dry lips, on weary arms.

Even so, I weep.
My best was never what you desired.
To come close to your desire,
I would've had to speak the language of angels—
memorize their speech,
to show how deeply I longed for you.

But in every language I spoke,
you never understood
my love for you.

I must have collected flowers
for every time I thought of you.
Yet still, it was never enough.

Now I've run out of breath.
So I turn to the passage of time

and whisper in its ear to watch for you—
for I can no longer make you happy.

I have nothing left
to buy more time.

I surrender.

It was the end

though time doesn't end.

It only spins us dizzy on life,

until we forget to ask it to stop.

Bow to the sovereign

we beg or blame

lest we bruise deeply,

like a fig falling from its branch,

and the wasp finds rest in our flesh.

You break flesh for love only once

but that's a notion,

whispered by wounds

pressing fingers into cracked hearts,

shattering what was never whole.

Meet the mother of agony—

not heartbreak,

but memory:

a river beneath the skin,

intoxicating as wine,

it drives some to madness,

others to prayer.

But even atheists believe—

love is the last miracle

Still

they allow.

The beatitude we chase,
then turn from
afraid to mispronounce
the language of forever.

I have two choices:
bottle my tears
and set them on fire,
watch memory evaporate,
my chains fall free—

or I choose fig jam.
A sweetness denied,
spread across the wound
called love
the hurt
once named the half
that made me whole.

Burnt

lovelorn (adj.) — suffering from lost love.

Though I speak with tongues of man and of angels,

But have not love, I have become sounding brass or a

clanging cymbal.

1 Corinthians 13:1

Birdie,

still you sing

as you carry what's not yours.

You do not ask.

You do not look back.

But you are beautiful—

and I am learning

that beauty doesn't ask permission

to break things.

My mind sits behind the bars of this
world.
Woeful is time's passage,
chained to the depravity of a soul
who has never known love.

A string stretched between two hearts.
—Oh, but what comes of this?
Bound and unbound at once,
I feel the trap tighten,
until I say: sever the string's grasp.

To tear two souls apart,
on the belief that love is a stifler of light—
Oh, what a tragedy.

Yet, in another breath—
I hug the maple in your throat,
like a parasite to a tree:
drawing strength
even as I drain it.
Clinging to the fragile proof that love exists.

But in all things—despite all these
things—

To know love is to walk hand in hand
with sanity.
And now I come to you,
utterly consumed
by the fires of madness.

God rest my restless soul.

Burnt

I am undeserving
of laugher.
With a bitterness newly born.
Why must greed counter tranquility?
My soul wanted more,
but my being was content
with the scraps you threw.

I rage with strange admiration.
You were my whole subject.
But it brought me ill
when you became my sole
longing.

It festered like the pungent smell of
mildew.
I washed and washed,
but there was no rinsing the scent of
indifference.

The truth of this is miserably freeing,
humbled I was to admit:

when you threw me pride, and I desired humility.

I kissed your feet,

when you gave passivity, and I begged for assertion.

I blessed your efforts.

I was in shambles of rage and devotion.

These are the things I never got to say.

Alas, the object lies idle,

and our time together has been spent.

Burnt

I burned for you—

and you burned me.

Grief builds its nest within my bending knees.

I fall to the earth; the soil my only kin.

Alone, I beg the sky for silent ease,

Yet find no rest—just hunger deep within.

A moldy hope grows through my hollow bones.

My name decays, unspoken, and unknown.

A persimmon cast off for a name well-known,

Abandoned, like a corpse, abasing, alone.

I curl—an inward bloom of clenched regret.

A petal turned against the tomb of the sun.

My breath is ash, my body slick with sweat,

All warmth of spirit I must shun.

Let rot come swiftly, and strip away my skin.

That I may bleed, and cleanse myself from sin.

A story that brings me no comfort

is my love story.

Yet it is what makes me smile,

and will reign in my heart forever.

I drink truth but never has such thirst become of me.

I am parched.

Burnt

Our arms are the anchor to this dance,

guiding our bodies through the air of

sorrow

as a grand piano plays in minor—

yet,

we are ever so happy.

The room mirrors our love.

For they recognize the waltz of spirits.

I close my eyes, feeling your guidance.

Yet, the rain—

it soaks my gown,

floods the room,

waking me from this daze.

I am dancing a waltz,

as the piano sighs—

but I dance alone.

The one who holds me in a warm embrace—my

cardigan arms.

I hear the soft cries of Claire De Lune,

And I feel her. I understand her.

Burnt

I make art on
gray sheets.

I am losing my mind.

Howling onto my canvas,
water coloring with,
tears and drool,

Leaving a face behind—
a ghost to mock me.

An omen of how I will feel.
A ghost of myself without you.

You smack me with cruelty

and touch me with your lips

to kiss it better.

Burnt

Where you were

bitterness lies.

Intertwined together

in our bedsheets.

I cheat on you with resentment.

Taking all of my time,

capturing all of my attention.

I give it willingly.

We were torn apart

by necessity,

marinated in the sour juice of animosity.

Then why does it hurt so immensely?

I want to hate you.

I need to have a conversation with grief

about the fact that I can't stop thinking of you.

About how each night, my dreams are lit by the light

of your name.

I hate you—despise you—

for loving you.

Lying with the cherubs,

I have made my peace.

I look upon you with the early glow of
dawn,
the way light plays across shadows—
too early for anything but the white noise
of earth.

In the beginning,
we gazed with admiration.
By the end,
we faced a thousand oceans of regret,
with sorrow filling the gaps of time—
and pain—
thunder feared
when it called.

I am not a tissue—

don't use me once, then

throw me away,

grasping for another.

Burnt

I hold an umbrella above my head,

there's a leak in my house.

I call a plumber to fix

the constant,

Drip. Drip. Drip.

Like two kids splashing through puddles,

we follow the trail of water,

umbrellas in hand.

We check every wall,

every tap,

every room.

He looks at me like I'm insane,

the trail of water leads to dry walls.

I flail my arms,

Keeping him from leaving me with

no answers—

wailing,

like a prophet once wailed,

a flood would soon come from the desert.

Boiling Point

There's a leak in my house,
no denying it.
I shoo the plumber out
with the tip of my red umbrella,
sliding down my door,
feeling very blue.

I cup my face in my hands,
wiping my eyes—
I do have a leak in my house,
I realize.

As my cupped hands fill with salty tears,
Drip. Drip. Dripping.
Steady down my face.

Burnt

Of all the ways to kill a person,

love—is the cruelest.

Indelible

in'deləb(ə)l

(adj.) Impossible to erase or forget.

(You have left an *indelible* mark on my heart.)

Burnt

Latin is beauty—

yet it is lost.

Love is beauty—

yet it is not.

Still,

we wander with lanterns

in the night.

Love is not savage.

It is kind.

If it is not,

it is not love.

Anger is not what I was prescribed,

but it's the substance I'm abusing.

Watch the match wilt.

Set the curtains ablaze.

Tuck yourself into bed.

Let your tears fall

at the feet of fire.

Do not fear death by flame—

fear drowning.

Dry your cheeks

with scorched tissue.

Pray the fire drinks every drop.

Let it quiet

the howl of lost love.

Memories drift like ash—

too cruel to keep.

Let it smolder.

Let the fire take pity.

If it reads your words,

may it love you.

Burnt

May your truth save you—
or burn with the rest.

Flames are cruel to the faint.

Ask for mercy when the fire

you lit rises

higher

than you.

You are the scent that turns heads.

—

I turn mine to weep.

Burnt

Lips kissing me,

the same that curve hatred,

scream at me,

and love me.

You use your tongue to caress

and to cut.

The mirror isn't shattered.

My self-worth is—

shattered in a million pieces.

Burnt

Fall, river, fall—so slow your silver thread,
You trickle down into the mouth of groaning.
Your voice is velvet moss where truths have bled,
And memory clings where silent ruin lies moaning.

Fall, river, fall—I long to know your face,
The way you were before the fire came.
Before the sky collapsed without a trace,
And ash replaced the whisper of your name.

Fall, river, fall—I pray the Lord to hear,
To take my soul, laid bare beside your flow.
My lungs are clay, my body cracked with fear,
Still waiting for a flood I'll never know.

Yet even now, I can't help but call:
Fall, river fall—oh God, fall, river, fall.

There is no point in life than to love.

There is no point to live after love.

Burnt

Losing you like paper to the wind.

I run after you,

while you laugh and whistle,

watching my silly little dance,

of trying to catch you.

It is within us to feel sadness.

Within us to feel love.

Why must we feel both at once?

If only I could twist time,

hold you in my arms just once more.

I'd give everything for a second chance.

But time isn't kind to pleads.

Waves of loathing call to me.

I stumble into their waters—

they invite me in.

My breath fails with icy torment.

I let them take every last drop of me,

engulfing all I am.

Now I cry,

begging—

for someone to hear.

Scoop me out of the quicksand I mistook for shore,

suffocating as I sink into a vicious cycle:

I loathe my decision.

I loathe myself.

Descending into the depths,

only my soul remains at the surface,

rocking in anguished waves,

discarded, forgotten.

A dreadful death.

No note. No warning.
I leak into the waters,
still begging to be heard—
to be a lesson.

Don't fall into their waves.

But no one hears.
And day after day,
it becomes my duty
to catch their begging tears—
and invite them in.

A wise man's foresight of need—
a fool's despair in wasting away.
Yet both are undone by its hunger.

—

I'd have resolved to rot as the fool.
But I chose the wisdom of restraint—
and suffer just the same.

Your laughter is lace; your love, torn. You bear the
elegance of puffed sleeves. I wear rags, but in my dreams,
you are my embellished gown. A corset tightens around my
soul, taking what little I had to give, yet holding me whole.
Ruffles gather beneath my eyes.

—

With the color I choose, may you dress me in white—
though all I own is monarch black.

Present in love—

holding your heart through

pain,

celebrating the highs,

consoling the lows.

There to cleanse you

when emotions overflow,

spilling,

dripping,

staining your cheeks,

falling on dry lips.

You may taste

sadness,

joy,

fear,

or the worst of these—

love.

Or you may simply taste tears.

Burnt

If it is love that makes you cry,
let it not fall and stain the floor with pain.
Awful a thought for a seed to be watered,
with a tear of cruel love,
and, for that seedling to grow
and devour a field of roses.

Unfortunate should that weed overthrow
beauty.
Let that seed not consume your mind,
let it not grow to consume a field of beauty.

You stain like turmeric, and

settle on my chest

like wet cloth.

Answer me—

But don't give me an answer.

Tell me—

But don't let me know.

I cannot bear to hear you say

yes.

Tormenting our feet with shoes

grief filled with weight

it couldn't bear

and yet,

dared us to run.

Burnt

I wear bitterness like second skin,

the taste of your absence on my tongue—

I curse the moments we'll never share,

I wish for an escape from this relentless ache.

To my bones, I cry—
Lift me.
But it is my heart who hears,
my soul who feels.

Without them,
I am only a husk,
waiting
for death to invite me in.

Burnt

I claw at the world for taking what I couldn't keep.

I burn the edges of memories,

and shout at shadows that refuse to speak.

Light is captured,

then it goes on to capture your

moments—

a photograph.

It focuses on your breathtaking smile,

pure bliss,

failing to capture the heartbreak

lingering behind the flash.

Single. Sullen.

The photograph didn't hold

unrequited love—

only the tangible;

your glowing smile,

now erased

by misery.

I would shatter the lens

before I ever shatter

my heart

again.

Funny—

to capture a moment worth keeping,

one that glows in memory,

no camera is in sight.

Euphoria

only takes pictures

while we sleep.

Where there is illusion,

there lies sanity.

Washed up,

coughing and gagging,

as it was forced—

pushed into the ocean floor,

by the remnants of a life

full of laughter.

Where the curtain is never pulled,

and the sky never falls—

lo, it is a beautiful paradise.

Interrupted only

by the coughing

and gagging

of my sanity.

Burnt

The ashes in my soul stir,

hearing with quiet surprise.

Grief is capable of muddling

uncommon intelligence,

with the folly of its desire—

until what is true is unrecognizable.

—

If it doesn't stand the test of honesty,
it won't stand the test of time.

My two friends,

guilt and sadness

told me

it wasn't my fault.

Guilt lied.

But sadness didn't.

All she did

was cry.

Sodden soil catches petals,

and the wonderfully solid ground catches me. Like a rose,

my love for you has fallen away,

the ground littered with tissues.

Fossils of pain.

My aroma pulls you in forever more. Bringing you joy.

While I suffer with quiet thorns of misery.

First love, one can never forget.

Forget-me-not.

Selfishly, carelessly, I beg.

Oh rose,

a pile of broken beauty—

fragile with pruned slivers,

The Great Gardener with a green thumb and abundant

wisdom says,

prepare, for the season after last.

Mist tilled soil with absolution.

Cultivate new growth, Prepare for new sowing.

Alas, I do,

temptation never sterner, never stronger.

I hold tightly to the ground,

But I must let go

——

I must grow again.

The quiet laughter of sleep douses me, waking me,
drawing me into the cove of lies where you lead me to
silence. Knee-deep in darkness, cold seeps in, cloaking me
in a coat of sin to weigh me down. You press sand into my
mouth so I won't disturb our love. But I strip bare the sin
you placed on me and sink into the cove. Further, I
discover truth. Further, I dive—into myself— until my
mind becomes my narrow cocoon.

What the caterpillar calls the end, the rest of the world calls a butterfly.

—*Lao Tzu*

Boiling Point

It smells holy.
Cathedral bells sound as I sit
in viper-black silk,
mourning life before it leaves.
Threads whisper across my knees
as I sit politely on oaken pews of life.

Before me rests the absence of darkness—
lit in the fairness of peace,
comfortably seated
on pews of death.

———

We begin life at the mouth of
a slow river.
Stained Glasswing waits by waters
of dark, fickle milk,
the air thick with regret and rust,
waiting eons for us to fall
into mossy jaws of final stone,

and lie upon

118

plump lily pads—

dry.

———

Greta oto—cathedral in the skies—

lapsing through

hollow wind,

quiet—*whole.*

Like silk before it is spun,

before it is laid on soft silver scalps—

the torn flutter of a Glasswing butterfly

announces the arrival of a

proverb.

Sit with one.

Fly with one.

As you rise, lit in fairness,

thin-boned,

from the oak, hand in warm hand

walking toward pews

nailed before the

preacher's stand—

footsteps echoing

like breath in a tomb.

———

But before thin bones and warm hands,

we begin at the mouth of the river,

there the milk has not soured,

and rust has turned

clean,

The glasswing is in a cocoon.

There is no time yet

for regrets.

———

Let it be known.

One day I'll find my one along the river.

Not to bathe in silence,

but in life.

Not dry, plump.

Only then will I have peace upon death.
Perhaps, then I'll believe life can be a dream,
a dream within a dream.

———

And, if it is—let me find
them in it.
With them, I will sit.
With them, I will fly.
Sit with one.
Fly with one.
Glasswing.

Glasswing

Simmering

petrichor (n.) – the smell of earth after rain.

Perhaps, it is the lover whom you find beautiful—

brave, strong—

while they take what you had first.

They may take your *mind*, your *spirit*,

but the *birdie* is so beautiful,

so brave, so strong.

You wonder if they are *delighted*—

though they took what you hadn't offered.

Beloved.

It asks:

If someone I loved grows stronger by breaking me.

Am I allowed to find beauty in them still?

Am I allowed to mourn what they took,

even if they shine because of it?

It asks:

"Should I be delighted too?"

Tragedy tends the roots of beauty.

The early sparrow who pecks the earth for the worm

finds what it seeks—

all the while looking down.

The sky above us

holds the truth of the future.

Yet even the rain

falls to the ground,

pools for us—

as we look down,

to discover puddles

of mud.

If it is true that we must look forward,

never down—

why was grand truth

revealed to Adam and Eve

not by looking up at the tree,

not at the slithering

serpent,

but down—

at their feet,

at their nakedness?

—

You must look down,

so you do not stumble on sharp stone

and bruise your hip.

But when you rise from a sallow

fall,

paint your eyes to the sky,

to look forward.

In life, both are needed.

To take the next step,

worm by worm.

To take renewal as the sun takes

the day,

hour by hour.

—we say deep down,

while it rests on the surface.

Tormented by the waves of the day

you gave your all to the one.

Betrayal strikes you into viscously sharp rocks,

losing the most delicate part of you.

Taking you down, swifter than they declared their love.

To what end, will I love again?

To my wits end,

I ask, will I ever trust again?

Realize, the part stung by the waters salt,

shall seep into my veins and infect the love I had,

to whisper what I already knew:

I may never give my all again.

Despondently, I say,

the part of me I love—and evermore hate,

lives for you.

And what I fear more than the wink of death,

or mildewing darkness

is losing more of me—to you.

I'd like to carve it out,

but no knife is big enough

for the pain I feel.

— *Honesty*

Others, live to love.

Borrowers, live to die.

Once I believed I lived for you.

Now, I have not a clue.

What do you live for?

What do *I* live for if it's not for you?

Why does the willow weep?
Why has no one asked her?

Her soul must be trapped,
rooted,
growing in the branches.
Maybe she was once a lovelorn girl,
buried beneath heartbreak.
Now she weeps for all to see.

Can you hear her,
accompanied by the wind?
The forbidden howl of a soul
tormented by love's unforgiving grasp.
Oh, no one should face weeping alone.
Did one very lonely girl
pass over into the soil?
Was she undone by her hands—
or by shadows not her own?

She must have craved love,
with the ground embracing her,
like the arms of an elder,
giving homage to her feathery long tresses
transformed into long, feather-veined leaves

—

a curtain of beauty,
as she bows her head in weeping.

With branches, long and slender,
her arms to hold her while she lay weak,
bound to endure her burdens,
too insatiable, too heavy to bear bleak

—

and so, she scatters seeds of sorrow.
A test to those who pass beneath her.
Which lives are kind?
To ask, to care, to mend the splintered.
Which souls are cruel?
To distort, disregard, and mock
the broken?

Perhaps she was the loneliest girl in the world—
and now, the willow weeps for her.

Or, perhaps they are both lonely, and together,
forever bound to
weep.

Expect to be loved,

the way you love yourself.

Don't smile at me
you are cruel.
Don't say you care
when you beg for another.

You look down on me,
demand perfection.
You want my love,
want me to be flawless,
But you ridicule me—
day and night.

Each time you look at me,
your eyes burn with rage.
You pick at me,
scarring me,
making me loathe myself.

I will never heal—
not until you heal yourself

— *Your reflection*

The ocean is no virgin.

Her rivers—offspring,

polluted and tossed.

The currents do as they please.

Salt-stained and sovereign,

she gathers her waves like hair.

With the bite of salt, she guards her skin.

Rise to touch her with reverence—

for I see tides in her eyes,

drowning something nasty inside,

hopeful for peace.

Saltwater that heals—she aches.

The hands that cast stones

forget the weight of being broken.

Therefore, you who are without sin—

cast the first stone.

And you who sin—

seek.

Seek atonement in her arms,

while she swallows your ashes,

gagging—

choking.

O tides.

Tides in her eyes—

drowning something nasty inside.

I weep,

I moan—

you must see.

Pray for the ocean.

Pray for her to be set free.

Midnight embers glow—

an invitation to warmth.

I once took bashfulness

for granted.

Now tragedy takes a tighter grasp,

and romance is cold

inside my soul.

—

My face is plain,

but my heart and words

dress leafless branches

in winter's snow.

I lack air and elegance—

yet that is what you say.

I am easy to love,

bequeathed with sense,

dressed in intention and grace.

With holy guidance,

I clothe my soul in light.

May I be Cassiopeia?

Or one of the fields?

No—

I am not as alluring to you

as azaleas to a hummingbird.

Yet I gather the dew

of morning's love, like the calla lily.

I spin upright webs,

as widows do with their bellies of red.

I spill the fragrance

of an effervescent life—

like rosemary

laid down in an open field.

If I am meek, or simple,

at least I have the earth

singing my name.

Let me simply say:
I loved you.

I loved you in the way
trees love light—quietly, and to
death.

Remember:

hour by hour.

i

I left the window open,
hoping your memory might return with the wind—
the same wind that once carried your brilliance,
that heavy, aching radiance you left behind.

———

iv

In my mind, you are a kite:
weightless, drifting, unreachable.
Soaring effortlessly.
And I remain tethered to the ground,
holding a string that's long since frayed.

———

i

The truth settles inside me like roots
burrowing into hardened soil.
I tried to plant lies in my chest—
sweet ones,

the kind that bloom in denial—
just to keep you alive
a little longer.

———

iv

Sometimes I close my eyes,
pretend I hear us—
faint echoes that shadow me
like a sky of swollen clouds.

And in those clouds,
I am tempted to believe—
but clouds are just clouds.

———

i

You've become a prism of light:
refracted,
untouchable.
And I—your captor—

142

still clinging to what once was.

———

iv

Release me.

Close the window.
Let the scent of desire rot in the breeze.
Though I remain,
yearning for your touch,
the wind I suffer is my own.

———

i.

And you—
you will always be
my kite in the wind.

I choose to honor myself.

In doing so, I honor life.

Simmering

Long ago, I was slain by life.
Ripped into jagged flesh,
tilling the soil of my bones.
I reaped agony—
and sowed a seed.

Now, I water my tree.
With a noose around my neck,
I wander,
watering my tree.

I shall sit among the stones,
only to be understood, what it is to be
tossed and forgotten
Water.
Breath should belong to the skies,
not myself, not my lungs.
Water.
I stain the earth with sorrow even the rain
cannot cleanse.
Water.

My tormented tree will grow tall—
tall enough to hang me one day.
All it takes is time.
And water.

Look down.

Let the palm of your hand dirty—

for our hands are only dirty when we

grow.

Then look forward.

—

Steps and steps.

Most days I feel nothing.

Before that, I felt something.

and before—

I felt everything.

Even the loveliest things remember

sorrow.

Simmering

You retest my soul beneath shifting light,
questioning why I feel so foreign to you.
You dig deeper,
searching for a leak of love I never patched.

But look no further than my eyes—
they speak in waves,
so honest and true.

You mapped a course for my life,
but the waters were far too strong to
steer.
Shame on me
for believing you authored fate.

I may have sunk,
but the truest Author wrote:
you'll cling to the raft of forgiveness,
and grow with the splitting cold of age.

Settling is for materials lost to erosion.

I told a soul I loved them—
now I wander deserts.
Dry winds stripping my flesh of hope,
parched by a drought of love.

All I beg—
kneeling to grains of sand—
is this:
have you found a patch of lavish water
pure enough to quench me?

But all I taste is burnt earth,
a murky flask raised to my narrow lips—
and still—no drop of change spills.
My spirit finds no comfort here.

I lie dehydrated by hurt,
wrinkled by sorrow,
longing to be a vineyard of grapes,
bloated with passion.

So I lament to dry lands,

lifting my flask to swollen clouds—

I endure the torture
for a glimpse of paradise.

Some don't survive the drought.
But those who dare,
and lift their flask to heavens,
heal at the sound of rainfall.

Daylight to daylight.

There's an unwelcome presence
curling in the brink of my mind
where I go to tempt longing.

To feel death's breath on my cheek
as I go to my edge.

It hits me—
I have grow glass instead of moss.

I converse with life.

She tells me the things I despair to hear

but she tells me with prickly pear truth

coated without thorns of remorse

and that is why she is

my favorite.

When I'm blessed with a new flower,

never shall it wither.

I wish I did break.

But I have not.

I wish I did not heal.

But I have.

I say I wish,

because it almost broke me—

the straw

that nearly broke the camel's back—

was choosing myself.

For who am I?

That question,

the anchor pulling me into darkness,

but with my dying breath,

with all I had left in my lungs,

I screamed to wake myself from grief:

You were once his—

now, you are yours.

Worm by worm.

Don't compare me.

That is the thief of joy,

and I just got mine back.

———

Time offers no excess.
My pail brimmed with life's water,
and greedily,
I begged it never to cease.

I thought I had no choice
but to love—

to love
with my eyes shut tight,

to love
though my thoughts burned
with warning.

But I had a choice.

Now I dance with a broken valve,
echoing laughter through its cracks,
and fill more pails
than my own.

In a shoebox, I tuck my past,

and let her drift

carried by the sea of tears I once cried for her—

Boiling Point

When a flower is too comfortable as a seed,
and tarries in shallow soil,
rejecting the light,
spitting out the water—

when a flower grows content
in a field of dry death,
then it, too, shall wither.

But, a flower that takes up root,
seeking fertile soil—
let it be known, that flower,
brave and uncomfortable,
will reap a grand fortune.

Even should it die
before blooming again,
its seeds will blow into a land of
milk and honey.

Let it be understood:
it will grow tenfold—
nay,
it will grow like a wildflower.

Simmering

I invite myself to the
eternally flowing body—
she carries a heavy current,
yet waters the lavender
dried across my soul.

I place my feet in the coolness,
letting her become one with me.

You can let it go,
she breathes into me.
Whisper to a rock,
let it skip from your heart
across my waters.

You don't have to be sorry.
I will always show you love.
The stones will catch your thoughts,
hold your tears.

Cleanse your soul.
Watch your sadness

sink into the depths—

captured by me.

I wipe my eyes

and whisper

—

thank you.

—

The erosion has passed,

the winds have tried to blow through me,

but it is a season too late.

Now my leaves are meant only for music—

a branch hollowed into song.

Renewal.

—

Hour by hour.

Steps and steps.

Daylight to daylight.

—

Worm by worm.

—

The bruise heals.

May we agree on this: happiness is finicky.

There is no vertical healing, nor vertical living.

We live on mountains of glory, and pain—

it is not black and white. I believe in the gray. And the

colors of life. I believe in Moonlight coexisting peacefully

with Claire.

The end of loneliness.
One's sorry end,
another's righteous beginning.

So tell me—
why are you so afraid?

Of falling, crashing,
or potentially surviving.

Surviving the past,
to begin anew.

Boiling Point

I was once asked—

"What were you dreaming about?"

But what if

all that we see or seem

is but a dream within a dream?

Love—

a dream worth dreaming.

Life—

the dream worth living.

Healing—

a dream you must dream within a dream.

This is my parable.

This is my summary.

...

I walked the line,

stumbling over my yearning sea.

I have borne my back into affliction.

I am moving, yet remain in position—

rowing and rowing into conviction.

Find me in the deep.

Not prolific, only discreet.

I have wept. I still weep.

Lay me with the souls I keep.

Down in the sand, they sing.

Rest me, please—I ask. I beg.

Let me give you this to bring.

You won't know till the final dregs.

Bound am I by life's crowing.

And yet, please know—

my back against the currents' flow—

and still—*I row…*

Thank you.

What a journey this has been.

—*Cilla*

BOILING POINT:
A Conversation With the Author

1. Which section—S*till, Burnt, Simmering*—
   resonated the most with your current or past
   self? Why? Was there a poem or line that
   especially reflected a moment in your own life?

2. The book opens with the question *"What were
   you dreaming about?"* How did your
   understanding of that question evolve by the
   end of the collection?

3. How does it compare to other poetry or
   narratives you've read?

4. What does the line "and still—*I row.*" Mean to
   you? How does that line echo through your
   own life?

5. Which poem stayed with you the longest? Why?

6. What do you think the title *Boiling Point*
   represents?

7. What do the quotes at the start of each section mean to you? *Some were personal, others borrowed— all intentional.* How did they shape the way you read what followed?

8. The poem that begins *"Fly, fly, little birdie…"* appears three times in different forms throughout this book. Why do you think that is?

9. If you could ask the author one question, what would it be?

10. Which section was your favorite? Why?

11. This collection invites the reader to interpret freely. Do you agree? Why, or why not?

12. What role did your own perspective play in shaping the meaning of these poems?

13. And lastly, by the end of the collection, which two emotions did you feel most strongly?

Acknowledgements

To my mom, for the last five years I've sat on the arm of our couch, watching you cook, learning about you, and life more than I thought I'd have the privilege to know. You taught me the hard truths, all while you chopped onions and sautéed garlic. I wouldn't trade anything for the years I've spent overlooking the woman who taught me what life had to offer; *only if you demanded the very best out of it.* You are the woman I am honored to know; the woman I want to become; and in a beautiful way, the woman I am today. There is no shortage of wisdom in your brain; you are never afraid of a challenge, so neither am I. Thank you for filling my heart with joy, my nose with your delicious cooking, and my mind with wisdom. I sat down as a child and walked away a woman. I love you.

To my dad, you had a torn rotator cuff at my birth, and I think in a way that encapsulates you perfectly. You have also hit your head many, many times, part for our amusement and part because you are so very clumsy. I think that also encapsulates you perfectly. But here is my dad: The clunking engine: that sound, and we just knew it was you coming around the bridge. Jonah and I would drop everything and run; we'd run to meet our best pal. When we got to you, you'd manually roll down your window and we'd jump into your arms, kiss you hello, run to the back, use the big wheel as a stepping stool, hop in the bed of your white 83' GMC, hit the side exactly twice, (that deep hollow sound, I'll never forget), and you'd drive us home. I know more than all those things that encapsulates you. The man your kids run to before they even see you. Thank you for the iconic memories. I love you.

To Jonah, you've taught me many lessons. You are my brother, yes, but you have grown to become my teacher. So what can I say right now except thank you. For wanting to be there for me always, for your honest corrections, for never forsaking me, and for being my first and truest friend. We have been through a lot together, and you have been my beacon of light through it all. I'm honored to know you—and call you my big brother. I love you.

To my best friends, Nicole and Ella. You both are a little too beautiful for this world. I love you.

To Austin Kleon, author of *Steal Like an Artist*—I binged your book on a rainy day in January 2025, a few weeks after my eighteenth birthday. Almost as soon as I finished it, I noticed raindrops on the window telling me their story. That day, I saw the world in a different light. I grabbed my notebook, clicked my pen, and wrote my first poem after four years of silence. Thank you for waking up that part of my brain.

And above all, thank you to the will of God. Years ago, I made a difficult decision that shaped my future. It caused me pain, and I rejected Him for years. But one night, I ran into His arms. Two years later, I felt a strong desire to write a book—any book.

What began as a children's book shifted when poems started pouring in—first a trickle, then doubling and tripling. One night, I wrote twenty-five poems between one and three a.m. The next morning, I knelt and pleaded with God to stop my words if they weren't His will. Five months later, here we are, because they were.

Thank you for answered prayers and relentless guidance with your gentle staff. I believe in You for the same reason You believe in us.

—*Love.*

Afterword

What you've read—
these are the things I've scraped the air to catch.

———————

Here are some of the butterflies I've caught:

The Monarch:
The worm, the steps, the daylight, that was mine.

The Swallowtail:
These pages you hold—
you also hold the water that grew my lavender.
It had to rain for that to happen.

The Pearly-Eye:
Some of it is grief speaking in metaphor. Some of it—
maybe all of it—is hope disguised as memory, or memory
dressed as hope. What I know is this: when we reach for
love, when we mourn what hasn't happened yet, when we
imagine peace at the end of the river—we are already
becoming. And, maybe that's enough.

The Painted Lady:
If you hated it, that's okay, too.
I disliked a lot of things for a long time.
That usually meant they were too close
to the truth I'd buried.
Or maybe—I just didn't like it.
That's also good.

So with that—

The Pipevine:
You should know something else—
something I learned about myself along the way:

I dream a lot.
I write a lot.
And in between those two things—
I live.

———

Gratias ago tibi.
Thanks, I give to you.

Priscilla Hadley is a poet, artist, and entrepreneur. At eighteen, she wrote, edited, designed, and self-published her debut poetry collection, *Boiling Point*. Born near the mountains of Colorado, she now settles on the hills of Central Texas. Writing is her calling. The world is her passion. To poetry, she is forever grateful—for the sweet honey of words.

Take this kiss upon the brow!
And, in parting from you now,
Thus much let me avow:
You are not wrong who deem
That my days have been a dream;
Yet if hope has flown away
In a night, or in a day,
In a vision, or in none,
Is it therefore the less gone?
All that we see or seem
Is but a dream within a dream.

I stand amid the roar
Of a surf-tormented shore,
And I hold within my hand
Grains of the golden sand--
How few! yet how they creep
Through my fingers to the deep,
While I weep--while I weep!
O God! can I not grasp
Them with a tighter clasp?
O God! can I not save
One from the pitiless wave?
Is *all* that we see or seem
But a dream within a dream?

—Edgar Allen Poe

A Dream Within a Dream